SUMMARY
of
THE CODE OF THE EXTRAORDINARY MIND

A FastReads Summary with Key Takeaways & Analysis

NOTE: The purpose of this FastReads summary is to help you decide if it's worth the time, money and effort reading the original book (if you haven't already). FastReads has pulled out the essence with commentary and critique—but only to help you ascertain the value of the book for yourself. This summary is meant to be a supplement to, and not a replacement for the original book

---

Follow this link to purchase a copy of the original book on Amazon.

TABLE OF CONTENTS

BOOK OVERVIEW

In this book, Vishen Lakhiani explores what makes successful people extraordinary and reveals ten laws anyone can use to make the radical transformation to a fulfilling life. In the author's view, the journey towards an extraordinary life begins with an awareness of the powerful influences that culture has on the self. The journey involves discarding outdated models of reality, taking on new empowering models, learning to be happy in the present, and crafting a vision for the future. Through this vision, extraordinary minds find their quest and begin changing the world.

This book is a combination of Lakhiani's philosophy and the life experiences of brilliant thinkers and creators who have achieved greatness in their own lives. It touches on the limiting beliefs that constrain people from living their lives to the fullest. As epitomized by his journey from growing up in Malaysia to running a million-dollar human transformation company, Lakhiani maintains that anyone can begin applying these laws in his or her life today and live an extraordinary life.

INTRODUCTION

When he was thirty-three years old, Vishen Lakhiani was invited to speak at an event in Calgary, Alberta. He shared the stage with, among others, the Dalai Lama, Sir Richard Branson and the former president of South Africa F.W. de Clerk. He spoke about goals, happiness and what it means to have an extraordinary life. Despite getting a spot reserved for the least popular speakers, Lakhiani was voted the best speaker by the audience. His hour-long speech garnered almost a half a million views on Youtube.

This book is the culmination of years of the author's research into what makes successful people extraordinary. In his view, there is a methodology that anyone can employ to have an extraordinary life. This methodology has empowered Lakhiani to turn his personal growth hobby into a company with two million subscribers and half a million students.

Lakhiani concedes that most of his life was by no means extraordinary. He grew up in Malaysia before moving to the United States, and he struggled with self-esteem issues most of his life. He confesses that he came close to flunking in campus, got fired twice, and failed in over a dozen start-up ideas.

Before he succeeded with Mindvalley – a million-dollar human transformation company – Lakhiani had to make drastic changes to his models of reality. He attributes his success to one skill that has served him over the years – his ability to take in new knowledge from all types of people, identify patterns in this knowledge, and devise new models for decoding the world.

This book presents ten of the dots Lakhiani has connected to achieve an extraordinary life. Each of the four parts of the book assesses a different level of the extraordinary code while each of the ten chapters describes a law that can lead you to an extraordinary life.

PART 1: LIVING IN THE CULTURESCAPE: HOW YOU WERE SHAPED BY THE WORLD AROUND YOU

The culturescape is a mass of human thoughts, beliefs and ideas that saturates and influences your life in both conscious and unconscious ways. It influences how you work, worship, love and marry, and determines the parameters you use to measure your self-worth. While some beliefs and ideas are functional, others are unnecessary and limiting. The first step towards redefining your life is to question your culture's "shoulds" and identify the outdated rules that hold you back.

CHAPTER 1:
Transcend the Culturescape: Where We Learn to Question the Rules of the World We Live In

While Lakhiani was growing up in Malaysia, his parents and educators impressed upon him that smart kids were meant to become engineers, lawyers or doctors. The prevailing belief was that these were the practical and realistic careers to pursue. This notion pushed him to study electrical engineering and computer science at the University of Michigan, even though his interest was in photography and the performing arts.

Although he managed to secure a job as an intern at Microsoft during its heyday, Lakhiani had a disorienting conviction that he was trending in the wrong direction. A few weeks into the internship, he got himself fired and went back to complete his college studies. Looking back, Lakhiani reckons that quitting the internship was a smart move because in extension, it meant that he was developing the courage to un-follow socially approved life rules.

It's not Working

Lakhiani admits that there was nothing wrong with pursuing a career in computer science. However, a lot was wrong with pursuing a "practical" career he had no passion for. He cautions that settling for a job you have no passion for sets you up for a life of dispassion and mediocrity.

Today, the health, finances, love life and happiness of most people is inadequate because they subscribe to rules that suggest that the journey of life is static. Most of these preconceived rules are a bunch of "shoulds".

• This is how you should look/feel

• You should go to this college and major in this college.

• You should live in this city and take this type of job.

Knowing the rules to follow and the rules to break is if the first step towards living an extraordinary life. Circumstances may force you to a job you dislike to make ends meet, or live in places you abhor until you can afford your dream home – everyone bends to the pressure of a fast-paced society. The danger lies in blindly accepting that you must live by the preconceived rules.

The Dawn of the Rules

Researchers hypothesize that the Homo sapiens species owes its survival to its ability to communicate complex, survival-related information, preserve this knowledge, and pass it subsequent generations. Over millions of years, language has helped human beings invent solutions to problems, create tribes, develop guidelines for cooperation, and form cultures. Today, language transcends its purpose as a communication tool. It shapes what people see.

The Dual Worlds

Over time, the cooperation guidelines that early man's language set became the base rules that governed cultures. In turn, cultures opened up the mental and physical capabilities of human beings and subsequently accelerated development. However, this development came at a cost: excessive focus on rules created fixed judgments about how life ought to develop. Today, the line between the cooperation guidelines essential for survival and the layer of half-true beliefs that people have created to simplify the world is almost nonexistent.

Welcome to the Culturescape

On one side of today's dual world are hard universal truths – most of which touch on nature and survival. On the other side are relative truths that touch on law, religion, finances and personal happiness. These ideas, models and rules are relative because they are not true for all human beings. These relative truths, which make up the culturescape, surround and influence you from the day you are born. It is of little substance to the masses that most of these concepts and rules are dysfunctional and limit people's true potential.

"The world of absolute truth is fact-based. The world of the culturescape is opinion-based and agreement-based. Yet even though it exists solely in our heads, it is very, very real."

Some of the concepts that solely exist in people's heads but are still real include supernatural beings such as God, practices such as meditation, and even entities like corporations and states. Although these concepts don't exist in the real world, they influence people's lives in significant ways. Thoughts construct the world and empower or restrict the generations that take them up.

Stepping out of the Culturescape

When you begin to see that most of what you call life is made up of a system of thoughts and beliefs, you realize that every aspect of life is questionable. Understanding that society's rules were set by people who were no smarter than you – and that they are not absolute – opens you up to question and step outside the culturescape and, subsequently, take charge of your life. The rules may be real, but most are only right for people who want to live a safe, regular life. Most successful people owe their accomplishments to their willingness to question the meaning of their education, career, religion and other "safe" rules of living that others won't question – and their courage to break away from the culturescape.

Law 1: Transcend the Culturescape

The culturescape may keep you safe, but it does so at the expense of your personal and/or professional growth. When you break away from the culturescape and embrace the pain of life's dips, you acquire the learning and wisdom that leads to sharp rises in the quality of your life. Every bad experience leads to some significant awakening that makes you stronger.

Think about it: the only reason you belong to your nation and culture is because you were born in it. The culturescape makes you who you are, but it does not have to define your future. Expectedly, questioning the culturescape will anger the people close to you because you will begin to question their expectations of you. Your search for meaning may lead you to leave your career or business, or even end some of your personal relationships. But before you can challenge the rules of the culturescape, you have to identify your limiting beliefs first.

Key Takeaways

1. We live in dual worlds masqueraded as one – the world of hard truths (think survival and science) and the world of relative truths (think cultural beliefs and society's expectations.)

2. Relative truths permeate every aspect of your life and can significantly empower or limit you.

3. Extraordinary minds select the rules to follow and those to ignore and continually push themselves out of their comfort zones.

CHAPTER 2:
Question the Brules: Where We Learn That Much of How the World Runs Is Based on Bulls**t Rules Passed Down from Generation to Generation

The Lies People Choose to Believe

Your mental images of the world can change, expand or shrink as you interact with other cultures, opinions and ideologies. Most of the beliefs people hold are not a result of rational thought; they are the result of social contagion. These beliefs spread from one person to the next without sufficient analysis. Essentially, most of your decisions are influenced less by your rationality and more by the ideas and beliefs of your culture. Following society's ideas is not wrong per se, but following the masses inhibits progress towards the extraordinary.

Brules

Brules are baseless rules that people take up to categorize things and simplify their understanding of the world. You soak in these rules from influential figures as you grow up. They influence your choice of religion, career and relationships. Although these rules are convenient, they pose real dangers because they often remain unchanged for decades or centuries.

To live a life that is true to your needs and goals, you have to question every cultural norm that is not rational or that has been disapproved by research. Every aspect of your life – from your religion and traditions to your education and political beliefs – contains some Brules that you can question and eliminate from your worldview to live a life that is true to yourself. Some common Brules include:

• A college degree will guarantee your success. On the contrary, the number of people with no college degrees working for blue chip companies is on the rise.

• You should marry from your culture/race/ethnicity. By doing so, you'll please your family or community and compromise your happiness.

• You should subscribe to a single religion. Confining yourself to a single religion locks you out of the wide expanse of beautiful spiritual ideas out there and curtails your spiritual evolution.

• Success comes from hard work. This belief suggests work can't be exciting or fun, yet those who find joy in their work show more commitment and are more productive.

Masterful living means working in fields you enjoy so much that it does not feel like work.

Five ways People take on Brules

1. Through childhood indoctrination. People soak up most beliefs in their dependent childhood years. The malleable brains of children make them extremely receptive to beliefs, cultural practices and ways of thinking that are restrictive. Phrases such as "because that's the way it is" are powerful in convincing juvenile minds that some topics or beliefs are beyond reproach.

2. From authority figures. Caregivers, relatives, educators and friends pass on rules that may not serve your best interest. Other authority figures such as politicians misuse their authority to serve their best interest. A politician, for example, may create fear of an atypical social or religious group to garner support for his or her election.

3. From the need to belong. The need to fit in forces people to adopt irrational beliefs and trade in their individuality. Most social groupings act like cults – they relentlessly push people to shut down their right to question.

4. Through social proof. People often believe what others believe to save the time and energy of assessing the truth themselves.

5. Through the preservation of internal insecurities. In the absence of logical explanations for things that happen to the self, people manufacture rules that protect their fragile egos.

Make a Dent in the Universe

When you identify and challenge the Brules, people are bound to label you a misfit or rebel. Misfits are the people who embark on extraordinary ventures that can potentially change the world. Some fail. But those who succeed get a new label: visionaries. Extraordinary people seek a better world for themselves and others and don't let social or political bureaucracy derail their pursuit. They question every rule that constrains their vision.

Law 2: Question the Brules

To draw a distinction between the rules that serve your best interest and those that limit you, ask yourself these questions:

1. Is the rule based on positive assumptions about humanity? If a rule reinforces the belief that humanity in primarily untrustworthy, hopeless or bad, it is baseless – mostly because of the erroneous generalization it makes.

2. Does the rule promote equality and kindness?

3. Does the rule bother you? If it's a cultural or religious rule that makes you uncomfortable, discard it.

4. Is it a rational rule or is it a result of contagion? Dissect socially conditioned rules to determine if they serve you.

5. Does the rule advance your happiness? Ask if you pursued a career, took on a relationship or moved to a neighborhood to meet people's expectations or serve your happiness.

Life beyond the Brules will be uncertain and frightening; your family, friends and society will push back and do everything to get you to conform. When you stand firm and pursue your own dreams and happiness, the outcome will be worth every trouble.

Key Takeaways

1. People inherit most of their behaviors and beliefs through contagion, not choice. Holding on to beliefs that do not serve you severely limits your growth.

2. Discard beliefs that bother you, those that are not positive about humanity, and those that do not advance your happiness.

3. Extraordinary minds realize that most of the world runs on outdated rules. They question the beliefs that are not in line with their vision of the world.

PART II: THE AWAKENING: THE POWER TO CHOOSE YOUR VERSION OF THE WORLD

When you become conscious of the culturescape around you, you gain an awareness that enables you to filter the Brules, rise above the culturescape, and make your own rules. As your awareness expands, you grow into an extraordinary person. At this level, you determine what shapes and influences your consciousness, what you believe in, and how you learn, live and grow.

CHAPTER 3:
Practice Conscious Engineering: Where We Learn How to Accelerate Our Growth by Consciously Choosing What to Accept or Reject from the Culturescape

Conscious engineering is a lot like computational thinking. In computational thinking, you solve problems by breaking them down, spotting patterns, and solving individual parts in a logical and linear manner. The goal is not to create a static solution – it is to create a dynamic solution that anyone can use. Just as you upgrade the operating system on your computer to make it run faster and better every so often, you need to do the same for your consciousness.

1. Your Models of Reality: The beliefs you have accumulated since you were born are your models of reality. You took on most of these beliefs through uncritical imitation, not logical choice. Although these beliefs make you, they are not you; you can swap those that do not serve you with those that do. Your beliefs shape your personality and your perception of the world around you. As epitomized by the placebo effect, a change in your mindset can alter your physical form and your reality. Adopting new beliefs changes your body, work, love life, and your ability to make money, among other elements of your life.

2. Your Systems for Living (Your Software): You practice your models of reality in your daily systems or habits – the way you eat, exercise, work and deal with money. When you do enough self-analysis, you identify the systems that work, those that need tweaking, and those you need to send to the recycle bin.

Law 3: Practice Conscious Engineering

Your growth depends on your models of reality and your systems of living. The current models of reality are limited in that:

• They are shaped by the "reality" of the world – yet every aspect of culture is questionable and malleable ,

• They determine systems of living. Some flawed models of reality have been ingrained in the minds and habits of people for so long that society does not know how to start all over again.

• The lack in conscious and spiritual practices. Current models of reality emphasize the physical aspects of living – what you eat or drink, how you exercise or work – and neglect spiritual advancement.

At their best, social beliefs and practices – including current notions of education, marriage, work and finances – developed because they seemed like good ideas in their infancy. Real growth comes when you change your beliefs and upgrade your habits. When you make the leap to a better model of reality or system, you can't go back.

How to speed up your learning rate

Conscious engineering is a process change. To speed up the process:

• Understand the fundamental principles before digging into the details. The fundamentals of conscious engineering are the models (beliefs and practices) and systems (habits and routines) of living. Look for new models and systems in everything you read or experience.

• Identify the areas of your life that need consciousness engineering. The twelve areas of balance you to upgrade to achieve holistic growth are:

a) Your love relationship – how happy are you in your current status?

b) Your friendships – how strong is your emotional network?

c) Your adventures – how much time do you have for new experiences?

d) Your environment – what is the quality of your work and personal spaces?

e) Your health and fitness – what is the quality of your general health condition?

f) Your intellectual life – how much and how fast are you learning?

g) Your skills – Are you growing the skills you need to succeed?

h) Your spiritual life – how often do you meditate or partake in spiritual exercises?

i) Your career – Is your career or business growing?

j) Your creative life – do you partake in activities that boost your creativity?

k) Your family life – how happy are you with your family, parents and siblings?

l) Your community life – what contributions do you make to your community?

Key Takeaways

1. Like your computer software, your beliefs, habits and routines need constant upgrading to better serve you.

2. Your growth depends on your models of reality and systems of living. Adopt the models that empower you and regularly take stock of your performance in the 12 areas of balance.

CHAPTER 4:
Rewrite Your Models of Reality: Where We Learn To Choose and Upgrade Our Beliefs

Although you are well aware of some of your models of your reality, most models are hidden and unknown to you. These models are deeply embedded in your subconscious mind and often take some grand intervention or deep contemplation to emerge. A large part of the journey towards the extraordinary involves gaining an awareness of the models of reality in your subconscious mind. Unfortunately when you take on a limiting belief, it becomes true.

In your adulthood (as was the case in your childhood) your mind looks for meaning in every experience you go through. It simplifies these meanings – often distorting them – and uses them to interpret the world around you. Over time, these models become a part of you.

Other people's models of reality also affect your life, no matter how untrue they are. The expectations people place on you become self-fulfilling prophecies – as epitomized by the Pygmalion effect. The reality you model about the behavior of your family members, friends or coworkers becomes a part of who they are.

Law 4: Rewrite your models of reality

Extraordinary people are different from others in that their mental models empower them to feel good about themselves. These models also empower them to alter the world in line with their vision. You can help others develop positive beliefs by always asking yourself what belief the other person acquires from your encounter.

To model an empowering Brules-free reality for yourself and those around you:

• Make a list of five things you are grateful for each day.

• Every day, think about something you did or a quality you are proud of.

Practice this self-affirmation before you sleep or when you wake up. Self-affirmations help to heal the effect of the limiting beliefs you acquired growing up.

External models of reality

How you view the world around you has a significant impact as how you view yourself. Some powerful external models of reality that the author has picked up over the years include:

• Everyone possesses human intuition. Intuition helps you make better decisions – don't ignore it.

• Mind-body healing is a powerful phenomenon. Creative visualization through meditation can heal parts of yourself.

• Happiness at work increases productivity.

• Spirituality does not have to go with religion. A belief in God does not have to include the angry, judgmental being portrayed by most religions. You can create a religion that combines some inspiring tradition with your own individual inspiration.

To explore your external models of reality, write down the beliefs you possess about the twelve core areas of your life. Examine how you define your friendships, adventures fitness and work, what you expect from your love relationships, and what you believe is your role in your family and community.

Two tools to rewrite your models of reality

1. Ask if your model of reality is absolute or relative truth. Challenge models that have no scientific validation. These include your religious beliefs, parenting models, and even eating habits. No culture dominates the world – some other culture probably does the opposite of what yours does. Listen to your intuition and remember today's absolute truth may not remain the same in the future.

2. Ask whether you are creating meaning where there is none. People manufacture as much as 500 meanings based on the happenings of a single week. Ask yourself if the meaning you generate from an event is really true for every other event. When you regularly partake in this exercise, your meanings become less, you stop fretting over small things, and you improve your relationships with others.

Key Takeaways

1. Most of your models of reality lie hidden from you. For example, you may unconsciously harbor the belief that you are not enough. It takes a bold intervention from another person or deep contemplation on your part to weed them out.

2. People carry limiting models of reality from their childhood. However, with the right force, you can disrupt these models and experience massive changes.

3. Ask yourself what belief your child, spouse, friend or coworker will take away with every encounter you share.

4. Practice self-affirmation to give yourself the love and appreciation your inner child craves.

5. Adopt models of reality that empower you to feel good about yourself.

CHAPTER 5:
Upgrade Your Systems for Living: Where We Discover How to Get Better at Life by Constantly Upgrading Our Daily Systems

Richard Branson's system for creating billion-dollar companies is simple: find and hire people smarter than you, give them productive work, make them see their work as a mission, trust that they will deliver, and focus on the bigger picture.

A system is a way of doing things, repeated and perfected over time. Your eating and exercise routines, the way you dress, the way you handle your personal relationships – that's your system. Societal systems, some of which have become obsolete, include the current educational, political and business systems. When you treat your systems the way you treat your computer or smartphone apps – constantly updating to newer versions – your life improves exponentially.

Extraordinary people are extraordinary only because they continually refine their systems for living. To upgrade your systems:

1. Read a wide range of nonfiction books, attend conferences or take online classes. Find a practice in an area of life – like work, relationships or exercise – that works for others and try it.

2. Increase your refresh rate. Your refresh rate is the time you take to update or acquire new systems. Talk to people who are enthusiastic about a part of your life you would like to work on and set time-bound goals.

3. Assess the effectiveness of your systems of living periodically. Measure your gains and find ways to optimize your performance. Set a non-negotiable point below which you shouldn't fall – could be the balance on your bank account, a high weight limit, books you'll read each week, or the hours you spend with family and friends. Start a correction plan immediately you fall off your target and resolve to get a point that is better than the one you were before you slipped.

Prioritize self-discovery because it is a life-affirming tool. Seek feedback about your personal growth from friends and write down all the dreams you would like to pursue. Speed-read books that touch on your relationships, adventures, health and fitness, skills, intellectual life, career and other aspects of your life. Attend seminars, networking events and courses or any other avenue you can learn and explore new systems.

Law 5: Upgrade your systems for living

Extraordinary minds constantly set out to discover and optimize systems of living that apply to their life, work and soul. Their constant pursuit of growth is what makes them extraordinary.

Society has created a system where it is normal to wake up feeling stressed, anxious, fearful or worried, yet these feelings are the body's warning system. You can adopt healthy systems to free yourself of these feelings. Some of the transcendent practices you can use to escape this rut include meditation, gratitude, compassion and bliss.

Key Takeaways

1. Constantly question yourself and think about how you could do things better. Treat your life systems like your computer and smartphone apps – constantly update to the newest model – and experience exponential growth.

2. Step back and ask why you do a daily routine, and how best you can do it. Take a few days to read about optimized gym workouts, rather than maintaining the same daily exercise routine. Constantly look for new ideas and system

PART III: RECODING YOURSELF: TRANSFORMING YOUR INNER WORLD

As you discard the Brules that hold you back, you start to accelerate your personal growth. You reach a state where you want to do more with yourself and for the world around you. New systems of living have the power to dramatically raise your happiness levels and give you bliss. They allow you to create goals that are not influenced by the culturescape and, subsequently, bend reality.

CHAPTER 6:
Bend Reality: Where We Identify the Ultimate State of Human Existence

To recode yourself, you have to question some fundamental ideals endorsed by the culturescape. You have to question what it means to be happy and successful.

One of the keys to achieving happiness is to stop postponing happiness and be happy now. Happiness exists in your mind – you have the power to achieve it irrespective of your circumstances. Set big goals, but detach your happiness from their achievement. The quickest way to achieve your goals is to be happy during the journey. Bending reality means operating in the present – in a state where you have a vision of the future that pulls you forward but does not mess with your current happiness. You are happy pursuing your goal, not just happy when you achieve it.

Elements of bending reality

1. Being happy in the present: Find an enjoyable way to pursue your vision of the future and have a sense of gratitude for what you already have to be happy in the now. Being happy in the now means feeling fulfilled without achieving your vision. This state motivates you to work continuously without burning out and, subsequently, helps you achieve your goals faster.

To hack happiness, you have to first drop the if/then model (if I get this job or house or spouse then I'll be happy) because it pushes your happiness to the future, and often at the mercy of things that are out of your control. Pursue daily routines that allow you to be happy now.

2. Having an exciting plan for the future: All extraordinary people have a vision for the future that propels them forward. Your vision of the future must be free of Brules or it will feel futile when you achieve it. Create goals that are not centered on a certain kind of job, appearance of lifestyle.

Law 6: Bend reality

Extraordinary minds have a grand vision of the future; the achievement of which does not affect their present happiness. This approach moves them towards their vision faster because they have great fun along the way. When you're bending reality, there is no demarcation between work and play. You work effortlessly because your mind is attuned to your vision of the future. This is the ultimate state of human existence.

Key Takeaways

1. Stop postponing your happiness. Be happy about who you are and what you have now.

2. Pursue big goals, but don't tie your happiness to them.

3. As you can choose any model of reality you want, choose one that bends reality – one where a grand vision of the future propels you but does not affect your present happiness.

CHAPTER 7:
Live in Blissipline: Where We Learn about the Important Discipline of Maintaining Daily Bliss

Your brain is at its best performance when you are positive about your circumstances and your future. When you sacrifice your happiness for success, you are sabotaging yourself. To bend reality, you must learn to control your happiness level.

Short and powerful bouts of happiness can come from unique human experiences such as sex, closing a major business deal, or winning a competitive sport. A rare and more enduring form of happiness comes from spiritual awakening and growth. A more common source of happiness is meaningful endeavors, such as parenthood or a positive vision of the future. When you go through an exciting event, there is a base level of happiness you return to after the event is over. With blissipline systems, you can hack this cycle to enjoy higher levels of happiness each day.

Systems for advancing your happiness levels

1. Gratitude: Practice gratitude to experience exponential leaps in your happiness level. Practicing gratitude not only gives you a more forgiving attitude, but also increases your energy and social connectedness and decreases anxiety and depression. To make gratitude a daily practice, look to your past (rather than your future) and appreciate your journey – how much you have learned, the support you've received and the progress you've made.

To make gratitude a daily practice, start and end each day by listing five things you are grateful for in your work and personal life. Focus on how you feel about the people or events happening around you, and encourage people close to you to take the exercise with you.

2. Forgiveness: To achieve blissipline, you must learn to forgive. Forgiving everyone who has ever wronged you in any way lessens your stress and anxiety and improves your thinking and creativity skills. To start off, make a list of people who have wronged you from your distant past to the present. Imagine yourself in the moment of the painful experience each of these people subjected you and allow yourself to relive the anger and pain. Once you do this, ask how the situation made you better and imagine a bubble of compassion surrounding the person who wronged you.

3. Giving: Practicing gratitude leads to giving, and giving leads to happiness. Giving not only gives you a greater sense of meaning, but also lifts your spirit and that of the receiver. Any form of kindness equates to giving: smiling to a stranger, helping out with a project, or giving someone an appreciation note. You can give love, ideas, compassion, energy, skills and even compassion.

Law 7: Live in Blissipline

Extraordinary people find happiness in their present and use it to fuel their vision of the world.

Key takeaways

1. Happiness increases your productivity and your learning curve.

2. To find happiness, look to your past – rather than your future – and take stock of what you have achieved so far.

3. Stand and end each day by listing or thinking about five things you are grateful for in your personal and work life.

CHAPTR 8:
Create a Vision for Your Future: Where We Learn How to Make Sure That the Goals We're Chasing Will Really Lead to Long-Term Happiness

Dreams, goals or aspirations create meaning in your life and thrust you forward. Getting bolder and better at setting goals places you on the path of the extraordinary. Conventional goal setting (which is all about pursuing safety) does not lead you on an extraordinary path – it only leads you to a futile pursuit of the Brules of the culturescape. The modern system of goal setting is fundamentally flawed because it confuses means gaols with end goals.

Choose end goals, skip means goals

College majors, careers and other life paths are a means to an end. Goals centered around achieving an income level or being with a particular person are means goals. These goals are misleading because they do not bring any real happiness upon achievement. End goals bring joy by themselves; they are about being truly happy, making positive changes to community, and experiencing love. End goals are the goals you pursue without the expectation of material reward or societal recognition. They are the goals that make your life enjoyable and meaningful and set you on the path of the extraordinary.

The most prominent distinction between these two types of goals is that means goals do not stand alone but end goals do. Means goals have a "so" in them. These goals are often about conforming to societal expectations or Brules. End goals are about pursuing your most intimate desires. These goals are mostly about feelings – the pursuit of happiness, love or other emotion. Working for them energizes you and time flies without you realizing it. To set end goals, ask yourself these three questions:

1. What experiences do you want to live through – in your love relationships, friendships, adventures and environment?

2. How do you want to grow – in your health and fitness, intellectual and spiritual life, and skills?

3. What contributions do you want to make – in your creative, family and community life and career?

When writing your responses to these questions, keep them simple, go with your intuition, and focus on ends. When you come up with a list of visions and aspirations for your experiences, growth and contribution, pin it on a wall where you can easily see it and refill the motivation you need to work towards your goals each day.

Law 8: Create a vision for your future

Extraordinary minds create visions for their future that are free of societal expectations. These visions center on end goals and revolve around what makes them happy.

Key Takeaways

1. Think of your end goals, rather than your means goals (such as a career or business) and let your career or venture find you.

2. Set goals that revolve around the aspirations you have for your experiences, personal growth, and contributions to your career, family and community.

PART IV: BECOMING EXTRAORDINARY: CHANGING THE WORLD

Extraordinary minds are fueled by a calling to change the world they live in. They strive to create new ideas and models that shake the culturescape and move others.

CHAPTER 9:
Be Unfuckwithable: Where We Learn How to Be Fear-Proof

Being spiritual does not necessarily mean resigning oneself from the world – it means rising above the world and challenging the status quo. A spiritual person can have insurmountable possessions or intimate love relationships. What he must do is transcend his fear of loss (of people and goals) by detaching his happiness and self-worth from what he has.

To rise above your own fear, your feelings of love and fulfillment must come from within yourself. Being unfuckwitable means attaining a state where external negativity does not affect you because you are at peace with yourself.

Law 9: Be unfuckwithable

Extraordinary minds have an internal validation system. They are at peace with themselves and their environment – untouched by the noise of other people's criticism or praise.

There are certain systems that can help you become unfuckwithable:

1. Self-fueled goals: When you have complete control over a goal such that no event or person can take it away from you, you have a self-fueled goal. Rather that setting a goal of being in love with someone, for example, you decide to aim to be constantly surrounded by love. Self-fueled goals free you from depending on others and from the sense of powerlessness that ensues. When you set these goals, your mind pushes you towards opportunities for achieving them. Failure cannot derail you because everything is within your control. There really is no loss, and you are free to live on your own terms.

2. Realizing you are enough: It is almost impossible to get out of childhood without a person acquiring the belief that he or she is not enough. Because of this, most people go through life trying to prove that they are enough. The result is a chronic dependence on external validation. In the absence of this validation, one starts blaming others for the circumstances of his or her life. Symptomatic statements include "my boss is a jerk" and "my spouse is inconsiderate."

To be unfuckwithable, you have to learn to stop seeking external validation and to stop judging people when they don't give you what you want. You have to become immune to the behavior, judgment and criticism of others. Knowing that you are enough gives you the courage to try new things and do more.

While you can't control the words or actions of other people, you can control your reaction to them. Resist the urge to prove that you are enough and learn to view people's judgment and criticism as nothing more than an expression of the things they fear in themselves.

To become truly unfuckwithable, practice these exercises:

1. Practice self-love: Look into your eyes on the mirror and say "I love you." Do this every day after brushing your teeth.

2. Make a daily list of three to five things you love about yourself.

3. Focus on your surroundings and on the present. Pay attention to your breathing for a few seconds whenever you feel distracted or tense.

Key Takeaways

1. Set goals that no one and nothing can take away from you. Doing so means you're happy even if you lose everything – because you are still an achievable journey that energizes you.

2. When you detach your happiness from the achievement of your goals, your fear of loss dissipates; you're free to dream boldly and act fearlessly.

CHAPTER 10:
Embrace Your Quest: Where We Learn How to Put It All Together and Live a Life of Meaning

The journey towards the extraordinary is an evolution.

• It starts with an awareness of the influence the rules of culture have on you and the realization that the world around you controls and shapes you.

• You move to the realization that you can choose and create the world you want to live in. You start practicing consciousness engineering where you dump outdated models of reality and take up new empowering models.

• You start connecting with the world inside you. Here, you learn to be happy in the present and set a vision for your future – the achievement of which does not affect your current happiness.

• You become unfuckwithable, find your quest, and start changing the world around you.

Finding your Quest

All extraordinary people share in the fact that they have a vision so big that the conventional rules and limitations of life cannot hold them back. They dedicate their lives to things they are passionate about and pursue callings, rather than careers. Pursuing a calling means pursuing ends that positively impact humanity or future generations. A calling excites you so much that working towards it does not feel like work.

To find your calling start by identify your end goals. When you are clear about where you are going, the right people and opportunities align themselves to help you get there. Two things will help move you towards your calling: Kensho (growth by pain) and Satori (growth by awakening). The pain from your failures or heartbreaks gives you tough love and resilience and forces you to grow. The awakening, which can happen anytime, gives you the courage to move upward. As the path will not be straight, it helps to remember that sometimes you have to tear apart a part of your life to let new things in.

Out of the dips and upward moves you experience, there's always a new way of life (your calling) trying to come out. Your calling finds you if you are awake – the more you create, the more the universe supports you. Be open to the intuitive insights that come as a result of your connectedness to the world and build your grand vision around these insights.

When you fail to reach your goals, it may be because these goals are not aligned with your calling. In every failure there is a question you need to ask yourself. In the answer to this question is a new model or vision worth considering.

Law 10: Embrace your quest

Extraordinary minds are driven by a desire to make positive changes in the world – a quest or calling that gives their lives meaning and enables them to contribute to the world around them.

To get started on your quest, you have to let go of the Brules that hold you back. In particular, you have to remember that:

• You don't have to be an entrepreneur. Entrepreneurship is a means goal, not an end goal. The end goal is a purpose you can get by working for companies with whose mission you identify. Start with a mission and ask what means will get you there.

• You don't have to settle for just any career. You need to be in a career that is right for you. Find a company that matches your mission and adds value to the world – one that is not just in business for profit.

Remember that your quest does not have to save the world; it merely needs to preserve it for the next generation. To identify your calling, ask these questions:

1. What has ever made you experience heaven on earth?

2. If you had a magic wand that could create heaven on earth, what would you create?

3. What easy steps can you take to create your heaven on earth in the next 24 hours?

Follow your intuition as you write your answers to these questions and pay attention to your feelings as you do so. The journey may not be easy when you take the plunge. When the dips become frequent, persistence will make all the difference. If you are not sure what to do, just take a tiny step to the direction your intuition shows you. That tiny step will give you the feedback you need for the next step, and your journey will be underway.

Key Takeaways

1. Let your intuition guide you as you set your end goals. Don't fuss about the HOW as this will limit you. Focus on the WHAT and WHY.

2. Find your quest, not your career, and you will find true greatness.

3. Taking on a calling to change the world around you gives your life unmatched meaning and makes work feel like play.

END

If you enjoyed this summary and analysis, please leave an honest review on Amazon.com…it'd mean a lot to us!

If you haven't already, we encourage you to purchase a copy of the original book.

12131926R00021

Printed in Great Britain
by Amazon